MEDITERRANEAN

DIET

COOKBOOK

The Complete Guide Quick & Easy
Recipes to build healthy habits.

APPETIZERS

EVA MILES

monetary loss due to the information herein, either directly or indirectly.

Respective authors own all copyrights not held by the publisher.

The information herein is offered for informational purposes solely and is universal as so. The presentation of the information is without contract or any type of guaranteed assurance.

The trademarks that are used are without any consent, and the publication of the trademark is without permission or backing by the trademark owner. All trademarks and brands within this book are for clarifying purposes only and are the owned by the owners themselves, not affiliated with this document

TABLE OF CONTENTS

APPETIZERS 7

1. Crispy Ring Onions 8

2. Stuffed Zucchini Boats 12

3. Tasty Harissa Sauce 16

4. Avocado Flavored Hummus 20

5. Gorgonzola Dip 23

6. Beet Creamy Hummus 26

7. Mediterranean Eggplant 29

8. Kielbasa Appetizer 32

9. Lebanese Style Hummus With Tahini 34

10. Feta Dip Mediterranean-Style 37

11. Tuna Capellini 40

12. Herb And Feta Dip 43

13. Tuna Pizza 46

14. Ginger-Turmeric Tahini Dip 49

15. Mediterranean Nachos 52

16. Mediterranean Appetizer Platter 55

17. Onion Kalamata Dip 58

18. Mediterranean Tapenade 61

19. Mediterranean Summer Tomatoes 64

20. Spinach-Walnut Greek Yogurt Dip 67

21. Cheddar And Bacon Dip 70

22. Mushroom Dip.................................73

23. Artichoke And Skinny Spinach Dip.....................76

24. Vegan Ranch Dressing.........................79

25. Mediterranean Chestnut.........................82

26. Zhoug Spicy Cilantro-Flavored Pesto 85

27. Lime Jalapeno Dip.........................88

28. Whole-Wheat Pizza.........................91

29. Cilantro-Peanut Dip 94

30. Avocado Corn Dip 97

1. Crispy Ring Onions

Total Time: 30 minutes

Difficulty Level: low

Servings: 4

Ingredients:

- 2 cups of buttermilk, divided
- 2 large onions
- One tablespoon of Olive Oil extra-virgin
- 1/2 teaspoon of each pepper, paprika, seasoning salt, and parsley
- 1/2 cup + 2 tablespoons of flour
- 2 cups of Panko bread crumbs
- 2 eggs

Instructions:

Peel and slice the onions into half-inch broad rings. Freeze sliced onions and 1 cup butter for at least half-hour.

Preheat oven to 400°F.

Combine the buttermilk, eggs, and two tablespoons of flour in a large mixing basin until smooth. Set the mixture aside.

Separately, add breadcrumbs, spices, and olive oil to another mixing dish.

Drain the onions completely from the freezer bag. Combine the onion and 1/2 cup flour in a plastic bag and shake well to coat.

To coat the onions, lay the panko combination in a small bowl and dip one onion at a time into the egg mixture and then the panko mixture.

Arrange onion rings in a single layer on a nonstick baking sheet. Bake for 20–25 minutes, or until crispy and browned, in a preheated oven.

Season the onion rings with more spice and serve.

Total Time: 20 minutes

Difficulty Level: low

Servings: 6

Ingredients:

- 1/4 medium chopped onion
- 1/8 cup of feta cheese crumbled
- Two tablespoons of pine nuts
- One teaspoon of dried basil
- 1/8 cup of diced green olives
- Six medium-sized zucchini
- One teaspoon of dried oregano
- 1/2 cup of grated Asiago cheese, divided
- Two chopped cloves of garlic

Instructions:

Preheat the broiler of the oven by positioning an oven rack approximately 6 inches from the stove.

Cut off the tips of the zucchini and cut each squash in half lengthwise. Scrape the squash seeds into a mixing bowl.

Combine the feta cheese, onion, olives, garlic, basil, oregano, half cup Asiago, and pine nuts in a large mixing bowl.

Replacing the zucchini shells with the mixture Arrange zucchini boats on a sheet pan and sprinkle with a little amount of Asiago cheese.

Brown the cheese for ten min under a hot broiler. Serve!

3. Tasty Harissa Sauce

Total Time: 15 minutes

Difficulty Level: low

Servings: *300 ml (over 1 cup)*

Ingredients:

- *Five cloves of peeled garlic*
- *1 x red bird's eye fresh chilli*
- *One tablespoon of smoked paprika*
- *5 to 6 tablespoons of olive oil*
- *Salt and pepper to taste*
- *1 x 400g can of chopped tomatoes*
- *2 x bell peppers red/sweet*
- *2 x fresh red chillies fresh*

For the spice mix

- *One teaspoon of fennel seeds*
- *One teaspoon of cumin seeds*
- *Two teaspoons of dried chilli flakes*
- *Two teaspoons of coriander seeds*

Instructions:

Toast all of the spices (from the spice mix) in a pan over medium heat until aromatic. After pounding them to perfection in a pestle and mortar, set them aside.

In a blender/food processor, combine all remaining ingredients, including the spices, and blend until brick-red and bright paste forms. Season to taste with salt and pepper, then transfer to jars.

4. Avocado Flavored Hummus

Total Time: 10 minutes

Difficulty Level: low

Servings: 10

Ingredients:

- One pitted and halved avocado (ripe)
- 1/4 cup of lemon juice
- 1/4 cup of tahini
- 1/4 cup of olive oil extra-virgin
- One can of no-salt-added chickpeas (15 ounces)
- 1 cup of cilantro leaves fresh
- 1/2 teaspoon of salt
- One teaspoon of ground cumin
- One clove of garlic

Instructions:

Reserve 2 tbsp. of the chickpea liquid and drain the remainder.

Mix the chickpeas and saved liquid in a food processor. In a food processor, combine the oil, avocado, cilantro, tahini, garlic, lemon juice, cumin, and salt.

Puree the mixture until it is completely smooth. Serve with crudités, vegetable chips, or pita chips as an accompaniment.

Total Time: 15 minutes

Difficulty Level: low

Servings: 20

Ingredients:

- 1 cup of sour cream low-fat
- 4 ounces of crumbled Gorgonzola cheese
- One peeled clove of garlic
- Salt and pepper to taste
- One tablespoon of fresh dill chopped
- 1 cup of mayonnaise low-fat
- Two teaspoons of unflavored gelatin

Instructions:

In a food processor, combine the reduced-fat mayonnaise, low-fat sour cream, dill, garlic, salt, gorgonzola cheese and pepper.

Blend on high speed until completely smooth. At this point, pour gelatin into the *mixture. Allow it to soften for approximately 5 minutes.*

Blend until smooth to incorporate the gelatin. Refrigerate covered and chill until ready. Serve.

Total Time: 10 minutes

Difficulty Level: low

Servings: 6

Ingredients:

- 15 oz. of canned and drained beets

- Kosher salt

- One small clove of garlic

- 2 ice cubes

- 2 cups of cooked chickpeas

- Parsley and feta cheese for garnishing (optional)

- Three tablespoons of tahini paste

- 1/2 teaspoon of each coriander, cumin, and sumac

- 1/2 lemon juice

- Extra virgin olive oil

For serving

- *Veggies*

- *Homemade pita chips*

Instructions:

In a food processor, combine cooked beets, lemon juice, chickpeas, tahini, and garlic. Season with salt and pepper to taste.

Start the processor and let it run for a few mins before adding two ice cubes.

Season to taste, adjusting seasonings as necessary. If the hummus remains too thick, pulse it again, adding more ice as you go.

Pour half of the beet hummus into a bowl. Drizzle the dish with olive oil. Spread parsley, feta cheese and over the top. Serve with handmade pita chips and vegetables of your choice.

Total Time: 20 minutes

Difficulty Level: low

Servings: 4

Ingredients:

- *Five chopped tomatoes*
- *Five peeled and cubed eggplants*
- *One tablespoon of salt*
- *1/2 cup of water*
- *1/2 cup of red wine vinegar*
- *Five seeded and chopped green bell peppers*
- *Five chopped onions*
- *1 1/2 tablespoons of white sugar*
- *1/2 cup of vegetable oil*

Instructions:

Combine the tomato, eggplant, bell pepper, and onion in a large pot. In a small mixing dish, combine the vinegar, sugar, salt, oil, and water. Distribute the

liquid evenly among the vegetables.
Bring to a simmer, then lower to low heat
and continue to cook for 25 minutes.

Kitchen Corner

8. Kielbasa Appetizer

Total Time: 30 minutes

Difficulty Level: low

Servings: 6

Ingredients:

- *One chopped onion*
- *1 pound of kielbasa, make 1/4-inch slices*
- *One jar of prepared jalapeno pepper jelly (10 ounces)*
- *1/2 cup of mustard*

Instructions:

Combine the mustard, kielbasa, onion, and jalapeno jelly in a slow cooker.

Pump up the slow cooker to its highest setting. Cook for 30 minutes or until the mixture is completely heated.

9. Lebanese Style Hummus With Tahini

Total Time: 10minutes

Difficulty Level: low

Servings: 6

Ingredients:

- 1/2 teaspoon of salt
- 2 cloves of garlic
- 80g of tahini
- 800g of rinsed and drained chickpeas
- One lemon juice
- Pepper
- Olive oil for drizzling

Instructions:

Pulse all ingredients in a processor until smooth if the batter becomes too stiff to mix, add a tbsp. of water at a time until the batter reaches the desired consistency.

Transfer to a mixing bowl and brush with olive oil, and sprinkle with additional salt and pepper.

10. Feta Dip Mediterranean-Style

Total Time: 5 minutes

Difficulty Level: low

Servings: 6

Ingredients:

- *3 oz. of softened cream cheese*
- *8 to 10 oz. of feta cheese crumbled*
- *1 Persian cucumber chopped*
- *Ten torn basil leaves fresh*
- *3/4 cup of tomato bits sun-dried*
- *Olive oil*
- *One teaspoon of honey*
- *1 1/2 tablespoons of chives chopped*
- *One chopped jalapeno*

Instructions:

Combine the feta, cream cheese, one tablespoon olive oil, and honey in *a large mixing bowl. Using the back of a spoon, gently press the cheeses together until they are creamy and well combined.*

Combine the other ingredients, including the two tablespoons of olive oil, gently.

Pour half of the feta cheese sauce into a serving bowl. Enjoy! Serve alongside pita chips or your preferred bread.

THE
SKINNY
FORK

Total Time: 25 minutes

Difficulty Level: low

Servings: 6

Ingredients:

- Two tablespoons of fresh parsley minced

- 1/2 teaspoon salt

- 1 pound of capellini pasta

- 1/4 cup of olive oil extra-virgin

- Zest and juice of 3 lemons

- One pinch of crushed red pepper flakes

- 1 (5 ounces) can of tuna packed in oil

- 1/2 can of cannellini beans (15.5 ounces)

- Two cloves of minced garlic

- 1/2 cup of grated Parmesan cheese

Instructions:

Bring a large saucepan halfway full of water to a boil, lightly salted. Return to a boil and cook the capellini for 5 minutes, or until soft but stiff to the bite.

Squeeze the lime juice into a large mixing cup, being careful not to squeeze the seeds. Incorporate the olive oil till fully blended. Mix Parmesan cheese, garlic, lemon zest, parsley, salt, and crushed red pepper in a large mixing bowl until well combined. Throw in the tuna, flaking as necessary and separating the larger pieces. Carefully toss in the cannellini beans.

Drain the capellini pasta and add it to the tuna combination. Toss to combine, then serve immediately.

12. Herb And Feta Dip

Total Time: 25 minutes

Difficulty Level: low

Servings: 8

Ingredients:

- 1/2 cup of feta cheese crumbled
- 1/4 cup of fresh mint chopped
- One teaspoon of freshly ground pepper
- One 15-ounce can of rinsed white beans
- 3/4 cup of plain yogurt non-fat
- 1/4 cup of fresh dill chopped
- One tablespoon of lemon juice
- One teaspoon of garlic salt
- 1/4 cup of fresh chives chopped
- 1/4 cup of fresh parsley chopped

Instructions:

Puree the feta, beans, yogurt, pepper, lemon juice, and garlic salt in a food processor until smooth. Add the herbs and purée until completely incorporated. Keep chilled. Serve.

13. Tuna Pizza

Total Time: 25 minutes

Difficulty Level: low

Servings: 6

Ingredients:

- One can of Tuna in Water, drained and chunked

- One chopped red onion

- Salt to taste

- One chopped Roma (plum) tomato

- One pizza crust, homemade or premade

- 2 1/2 tablespoons of olive oil extra-virgin, divided

- One teaspoon of grated Parmesan cheese

- 1/2 cup of feta cheese crumbled

- Two teaspoons of jarred minced garlic

- 1 cup of spinach

* *Two thinly sliced leeks (white and pale green parts only)*

Instructions:

Preheat oven to 425°F

Follow the directions on the package for preparing the pizza crust. 1 tbsp olive oil, drizzled over the top and sprinkled with spinach.

14. Ginger-Turmeric Tahini Dip

Total Time: 15 minutes

Difficulty Level: low

Servings: 8

Ingredients:

- 1/4 cup of rice vinegar
- 1/2 cup of tahini
- Two teaspoons of ground turmeric
- 1/2 teaspoon of salt
- 1/4 cup of water
- One tablespoon of fresh ginger grated
- One teaspoon of garlic grated

Instructions:

In a mixing cup, whisk together the ginger, tahini, water, garlic, turmeric, vinegar and salt.

Combine the remaining one and a half tablespoons of tuna, olive oil, red onion, *garlic, leeks, tomato, and salt in a small cup. Distribute evenly across the pizza crust. Serve with crumbled parmesan cheese and feta cheese and grated if preferred.*

Bake for 10 to 15 mins in a preheated oven or according to the directions on the crust package. Prepare and serve!

15. Mediterranean Nachos

Total Time: 10 minutes

Difficulty Level: low

Servings: 4-6

Ingredients:

- ½ bag of tortilla chips
- ½ of 14.5 ounces can (~3/4 cup) of garbanzo beans, rinsed, drained and patted dry
- ½ of a 10-ounce container of Sabra Hummus
- 1 cup canned artichoke hearts, drained
- ½ cup crumbled feta cheese
- ½ cup chopped roasted red peppers
- 2½ Tablespoons pine nuts
- Two tablespoons fresh minced cilantro
- ½ cup chopped tomatoes

Instructions:

Preheat the oven to 375 degrees Fahrenheit. Layer tortilla chips in an oven-safe baking pan, dollop with hummus and spread evenly.

Garbanzo beans, artichoke hearts, red peppers, feta cheese, and pine nuts can be sprinkled on top. Bake for 5 minutes or until the mixture is heated.

Take the pan out of the oven and garnish it with fresh cilantro and tomatoes. Enjoy!

16. Mediterranean Appetizer Platter

Total Time: 15 minutes

Difficulty Level: low

Servings: 12

Ingredients:

- 1 16 oz Hummus
- 1 10 oz Manzanilla Olives
- 1 6 oz Harissa or Roasted Red Pepper - Walnut Dip
- 1 10 Oz Marinated Artichokes
- One packet of pita bread, cut into triangles and warmed
- Assortment of cut Veggies like cucumbers, carrots and radishes

Instructions:

Arrange a large serving dish and a few serving bowls. Distribute hummus, red pepper spread, marinated artichokes, and olives among the bowls. Drizzle some olive oil on top of the hummus for an authentic touch.

Arrange the vegetables and pita bread pieces in an artistic manner around the bowls. Then, as needed, replenish and serve. As a base, you can mix and match the vegetables and pita pieces. Additionally, you can layer and fill the pita pockets to create an exquisite sandwich.

Bear in mind that there is no one-size-fits-all approach to creating and enjoying mezze platters. The best way to appreciate it is to share it and engage in lively, hearty discussion.

17. Onion Kalamata Dip

Total Time: 5 minutes

Difficulty Level: low

Servings: 16

Ingredients:

- 1/2 cup of sour cream
- One envelope of dry onion soup mix (1 ounce)
- Two cloves of minced garlic
- One package of cream cheese (8 ounces)
- 10 Kalamata olives pitted
- One red pepper roasted, diced
- 1/2 cup of feta cheese crumbled

Instructions:

In a food processor, combine the garlic, onion soup mix, red pepper, feta cheese, sour cream, cream cheese, and olives.

Blend on high speed until very smooth and well-integrated. Transfer to a bowl and chill for a few minutes before serving to let flavours combine. Serve.

18. Mediterranean Tapenade

Total Time: 25 minutes

Difficulty Level: low

Servings: 12

Ingredients:

- *2 rinsed anchovy fillets*

- *One tablespoon of fresh lemon juice*

- *Two tablespoons of extra-virgin olive oil*

- *8 ounces of pitted mixed olives*

- *Three leaves of fresh basil*

- *One clove of minced garlic*

- *2 tablespoons of capers*

Instructions:

In a food processor, blend the olives, lemon juice, anchovy fillets, basil, olive oil, capers, and garlic, scraping down the sides of the bowl as needed to ensure all ingredients are well mixed until the mixture has the consistency of a coarse paste, about 1 to 2 minutes total.

19. Mediterranean Summer Tomatoes

Total Time: 15 minutes

Difficulty Level: low

Servings: 6

Ingredients:

- 1/2 cup of olive oil extra-virgin
- Five coarsely chopped shallots
- Five medium-sized whole fresh tomatoes
- 1/4 cup of balsamic vinegar
- One loaf of French bread for dipping

Instructions:

After coring and slicing the tomatoes, toss them in the serving dish. Scatter the shallots over the tomatoes.

Combine the balsamic vinegar and olive oil with a fork and drizzle over the tomatoes.

Allow 5 minutes before serving, or store tightly wrapped in the refrigerator for up to 3 days. When the tomatoes are done, dip the loaf into the marinade and serve alongside French bread.

20. Spinach-Walnut Greek Yogurt Dip

Total Time: 10 minutes

Difficulty Level: low

Servings: one large bowl

Ingredients:

- 2 cups of Greek yogurt

- 1/2 cup of parsley chopped

- One clove of minced garlic

- 2 cups of baby spinach

- Kosher salt

- Pinch of black pepper

- Extra virgin olive oil

- One teaspoon of dry mint

- 3/4 cup of finely chopped walnuts

- One tablespoon of lemon juice freshly squeezed

For serving

- Homemade pita chips

- Veggies

Instructions:

Make a bowl of icy water and keep it handy. Blend the baby spinach and bring a large saucepan of salted water to a boil. After adding the spinach to the boiling hot water, cook for 10 seconds. With tongs, transfer the spinach to the iced water and put it aside to cool for a few minutes. Drain thoroughly and squeeze out any remaining water.

In a mixing bowl, combine the blanched spinach, walnuts, yogurt, garlic, parsley, lemon juice, and mint. Season to taste with kosher salt and freshly ground black pepper. Drizzle generously with extra virgin olive oil (about two tablespoons). To combine, whisk everything together. Season with freshly ground pepper and sea salt to taste.

Serve with handmade pita chips and vegetables of your choice.

21. Cheddar And Bacon Dip

Total Time: 10 minutes

Difficulty Level: low

Servings: 12

Ingredients:

- *One packet of ranch dipping mix (1 ounce)*
- *One container of sour cream (16 ounces)*
- *Freshly cut vegetables for serving*
- *Six cooked and crumbled thick-cut Bacon*
- *1 cup of Cheddar cheese shredded*

Instructions:

In a mixing bowl, whisk together the sour cream and dipping mix until completely smooth. Before serving, stir in the Bacon and cheese, cover, and refrigerate for a few minutes.

Assemble the dip by topping it with fresh vegetables.

22. Mushroom Dip

Total Time: 25 minutes

Difficulty Level: low

Servings: 4

Ingredients:

- Three tablespoons of mayonnaise
- 1 pint of fresh mushrooms
- One teaspoon of tahini
- 1/4 teaspoon of ground black pepper
- One tablespoon of garlic chopped
- 2 ounces of walnuts chopped
- 1/4 teaspoon of salt

Instructions:

In a food processor or blender, pulse the mushrooms until finely chopped and transfer to a dish.

Combine the mushrooms, walnuts, garlic, mayonnaise, salt, tahini, and pepper in a *large mixing bowl until evenly distributed. Serve the dip with pita bread or your favorite bread.*

Total Time: 30 minutes

Difficulty Level: low

Servings: 16

Ingredients:

- One package of chopped spinach frozen (10 ounces), drained

- Two jars of marinated artichoke hearts (6.5 ounces), chopped and drained

- 1 cup of Romano cheese shredded

- 1/2 teaspoon of lemon juice

- Two cloves of minced garlic

- One package of softened cream cheese (8 ounces)

- 1 cup of sour cream fat-free

- 1/2 cup of garlic croutons coarsely chopped

- 1/2 cup of Parmesan cheese shredded

- 1/4 cup of red peppers roasted, chopped, and drained

Instructions:

Preheat oven to 375°F.

Combine artichokes, cream cheese, Parmesan cheese, spinach, sour cream, Romano cheese, garlic, roasted peppers, and lemon juice in a baking dish. Croutons should be layered on top.

Bake in the preheated oven for approximately 25 minutes, or until bubbling and croutons are browned.

24. Vegan Ranch Dressing

Total Time: 10 minutes

Difficulty Level: low

Servings: 8

Ingredients:

- Five teaspoons of apple cider vinegar raw

- Salt and black pepper to taste

- One tablespoon of fresh chives chopped

- 2 avocados

- One tablespoon of fresh parsley chopped

- 1/4 teaspoon of garlic powder

- One teaspoon of fresh dill chopped

Instructions:

- Combine the avocados, parsley, vinegar, dill, chives, and garlic powder in the tub of a food processor. Blend *on high speed until completely smooth. Season to taste with salt and pepper.*

Total Time: 15 minutes

Difficulty Level: low

Servings: 15

Ingredients:

- 2 cups of soy sauce
- One can of whole chestnuts, drained
- 1 pound of Bacon
- 1 cup of brown sugar

Instructions:

In a shallow mixing dish, combine the soy sauce and chestnuts. Refrigerate for at least 30 minutes before serving.

Preheat oven to 425°F. Line a baking pan with aluminium foil and coat it with nonstick cooking spray.

Cut the Bacon into thirds using a sharp knife. Combine brown sugar and cinnamon in a small mixing cup. Once the chestnuts have been drained, sprinkle them with brown sugar. Each nut should be wrapped in a bacon strip and secured with a toothpick. Arrange the chestnut and bacon wrappers on the prepared baking sheet.

Bake in the oven until the bacon is crispy.

26. Zhoug Spicy Cilantro-Flavored Pesto

Total Time: 10 minutes

Difficulty Level: low

Servings: 6

Ingredients:

- 1/2 cup of fresh parsley packed
- 2 cloves of garlic
- Six sliced jalapeno peppers, sliced
- Salt
- 1/2 teaspoon of ground green cardamom
- 1/3 cup of olive oil extra virgin
- 1/2 teaspoon of ground coriander
- One lemon juice
- 1 cup of fresh cilantro leaves packed
- 1/2 teaspoon of cumin

Instructions:

In a food processor fitted with a blade, combine the jalapeno, salt, and garlic. Roughly chop.

At this point, add the cilantro, spices, and parsley. Process until smoother, thicker paste forms.

In a mixing dish, combine the cilantro paste and water. Then, in a mixing bowl, combine the olive oil, lemon juice, and olive oil. To combine, whisk everything together. Enjoy!

27. Lime Jalapeno Dip

Total Time: 10 minutes

Difficulty Level: low

Servings: 8

Ingredients:

- Five cloves of chopped garlic

- Four chopped and seeded jalapenos large

- 1/2 cup of mayonnaise

- Two tablespoons of milk, or more as needed

- One package of dry ranch dressing mix

- 1/2 cup of cilantro chopped

- *(1 ounce)*

- *1/2 lime juice*

- *One container of light sour cream (8 ounces)*

Instructions:

Pulse jalapenos, garlic, and cilantro in a food processor bowl until finely chopped, scraping along each side several times.

Now combine the sour cream, lime juice, mayonnaise, and ranch dressing mix in a food processor until smooth. Drizzle in 2 tablespoons milk gradually and pulse until the desired consistency is achieved.

Transfer dip to a bowl and refrigerate for several hours or until flavors have mixed.

28. Whole-Wheat Pizza

Total Time: 25 minutes

Difficulty Level: low

Servings: 4

Ingredients:

- One jar of basil pesto (4 ounces)

- 1/4 cup of feta cheese crumbled

- Two tablespoons of chopped Kalamata olives

- One whole-wheat pizza crust

- 1/2 cup of artichoke hearts, drained and pulled apart

- Two tablespoons of sliced pepperoncini

Instructions:

Preheat oven to 400°F.

On a floured work surface, spread pesto evenly over the pizza crust. Arrange artichoke hearts and Kalamata olives on top of the pesto, followed by pepperoncini slices. Serve garnished with feta cheese.

Bake in the oven for 10 to 12 minutes, or until the bottom crust is crisp and the feta cheese has melted.

29. Cilantro-Peanut Dip

Total Time: 15 minutes

Difficulty Level: low

Servings: 16

Ingredients:

- 1/2 cup of chunky peanut butter

- Ten sprigs of finely chopped cilantro leave fresh

- 1/4 cup of red wine vinegar

- Two teaspoons of fresh ginger root minced

- 1/4 cup of lemon juice fresh

- 1/2 cup of peanut oil

- 1/4 cup of soy sauce

- *Two teaspoons of red pepper flakes crushed*

- *Four cloves of minced garlic, minced*

Instructions:

Purée peanut butter, red wine vinegar, peanut oil, lemon juice, and soy sauce until smooth in a food processor.

Combine the cilantro, garlic, ginger, and red pepper flakes in a medium bowl.

Blend on high speed until completely smooth. Refrigerate until ready to serve.

30. Avocado Corn Dip

Total Time: 20 minutes

Difficulty Level: low

Servings: 8

Ingredients:

- One finely chopped tomato

- Two cloves of minced garlic

- 1 cup of corn kernels frozen, thawed

- Two teaspoons of vegetable oil

- Two teaspoons of pickled chopped jalapeno peppers

- Two tablespoons of onions finely chopped

- *Two avocados large pitted and peeled*

- *Three tablespoons of fresh lime juice*

- *1/4 teaspoon of ground cumin*

- *1/2 teaspoon of salt*

Instructions:

Preheat oven to 400°F. Combine oil and corn in a small pan.

Bake in a preheated oven for approximately 8 to 10 minutes, mixing once or twice until well browned. Allow cooling.

Mash 1 avocado and finely chop the other.

Combine the corn, mashed avocado, tomato, sliced avocado, lime juice, jalapeño peppers, onions, salt, garlic,

and cumin in a large mixing bowl; cover
and refrigerate until serving.